He's in the Midst of it All

DIANA STEVENS

He's in the Midst of It All
By Diana Stevens

Cover created and designed by: Jazzy Kitty Publishing
Logo designed by: Andre M. Saunders and Leroy Grayson
Editor: Anelda L. Attaway

© 2014 Diana Stevens
ISBN: 978-0-9916648-0-1
Library of Congress Control Number: 2014939754

All rights reserved. This book is protected under the copyright laws of the United States of America. This book may not be copied or reprinted for commercial gain or profit. The use of short quotations or occasional page copying for personal or group study is permitted and encouraged. Permission will be granted upon request. For Worldwide Distribution. Printed in the United States of America. Published by Jazzy Kitty Marketing & Publishing LLC dba Jazzy Kitty Publishing Utilizing Microsoft Publishing Software.

ACKNOWLEDGEMENTS

In pursuit of my passion, I found a secret treasure that laid dormant inside of me, and God pulled it out. I started writing this book. The topics were given to me by some of my close friends, family, co-workers, and each story was stamped with their approval. I wrote this book with a motive to inspire people to view God with a different perspective. I give thanks to Bishop William Martin, of the Pilgrim Church of Brownsville, who often prayed for me, and told me to write, and publish my work. I also give honor to Pastor Esther Banks, who was my writing Teacher at the Community Bible Institute at Brooklyn Tabernacle. She was the instrument that pulled out what God had already placed on the inside of me. I have included the story of a topic given to her by the Holy Spirit.

To all my friends and co-workers I extend my gratitude for all your encouragements and support.

I give honor to The Temple of Restoration whose presiding Bishop is Angelo Barbosa. Thank you, and your staff for your life changing prayers. Through all my circumstances, I was always able to reach out to The Temple of Restoration (T.T.O.R.), and always received a word of hope. I salute you all, and continue the good work.

DEDICATIONS

Growing up, my Mother had the strongest influence on me. She was my Mother and Father; she was my life coach. I didn't know what she was trying to teach me until life challenged me and I remembered all that she taught me. She had a funny way of using little stories to get her point across. It worked and it helped me through life's most difficult times. Mom was a great story teller and she expressed it in writing. I guess it rubbed off and fell on me.

My Mother is now presently with the Lord but I still hear her voice whispering in my ears *"Remember what I told you, pull it out and use it!"* A whisper sustained me during failing relationships, unemployment, and health issues. Most of all it gave me intuition when I didn't know what to do. My Mother, Father, Coach, Pastor, Nurse, and the giver of life to five children, is still alive and well. Everything she taught is what I use on this journey called life. Now that she not in this realm, I'm pleased to say Mom I hear you and dedicate this book as yours! Keep whispering your truths in my ears, and into my heart.

TABLE OF CONTENTS

Introduction..i
Chapter 1-A Passion to Pursue..01
Chapter 2-If I Can Say It, I Can Read It. If I Can Read It, Then I Can Write It..07
Chapter 3-Facing Our Fears...13
Chapter 4-What Can You Do When You've Done All You Can?..18
Chapter 5-Stop Dragging Your Feet!.......................................22
Chapter 6-Where is He When I Need Him?...................................27
Chapter 7-You Can Have What I Have!......................................34
Chapter 8-Do You Know What Kind of People are in There?..42
Chapter 9-In the Last Hours!...46
Chapter 10-Betrayal..50
Chapter 11-Why Are We So Easily Offended?................................54
Chapter 12-The difference in God and Man!................................58
About the Author...63

INTRODUCTION

This book is composed of short stories that were written to give the reader a different perspective of God. It contains stories such as, "Where is He when I Need Him?" It's a story based on emotions that we feel while we are going through extenuating situations. "How to Overcome Envy /Jealousy" is based on emotions that are uncontrollable but can be worked on if you see yourself the way God see you. This book is full of real life experiences, and emotions that occur in a Christian's life. It will inspire people with a Christian lifestyle as well as captivate those that don't attend church but have a strong belief in God. My motivation is to get people to see God in real life situations. These stories were written in simplicity so that it can be applied to the reader's life. It contains scriptures to relate to situations that can occur in ordinary people's lives.

CHAPTER 1

A Passion to Pursue

Who is that pregnant woman next to you on the train? Is she the new and improved Suicide Bomber that devised a method of concealing explosives in her belly? What can make a person create a new idea to inflict pain on not just themselves but millions? The culprit is Passion. Passion is the motivating force to create, improve on, and continue to do it even against adverse situations. But there is one passion that is placed in the heart by God to lead us into our destiny.

There are all sorts of passions in this world. Some are healthy, some destructive, while others are denied. But there is one passion that is placed in the heart by God that must be pursued.

In society today, there are many passions that are displayed all around us, passions in activities such as, biking, skating, fishing, and reading a good book. We can find people who are passionate for cultural foods such as, Italian, Chinese, Jamaican, Mexican, and of course, desserts. We can see in many of our parks, markets, and workplaces people who are passionate about each other. Others are passionate about the concept of religion, work, marriage, even in bad weather or adverse situations, we can find passion working in the background.

Today, we have a vast variety of multimedia technology that gives us a wider spectrum of passions in action. Television, movies, radio, and hand-held Internet devices give us a diversity of passions. Our televisions give us the News with topics of the new methods of warfare, pregnant cover-ups to conceal explosives. This is a passion of concept or belief in action. We go to the movies and are entertained with passions demonstrated, and entitled, "The Passion of Christ." We can turn on our radios and listen to inspirational stations. We can shop on-line and complete the transaction in seconds by the use of the World Wide Web. A passion is an intense desire for an activity, person, or a concept. It is evident that passion motivates us to create and improve on, for example, today's technology, weapons of war, and the civil rights movement.

Some passions are healthy for instance, jogging, swimming, and taking long walks. Healthy passions will produce results in reducing our heart rates, blood pressures, alleviating stress, and ultimately, reducing our weight.

These healthy passions give us the opportunity to reevaluate our lives, commune with nature, and with God. Healthy passions are good for the body, mind, and spirit.

In most settings today, whether at work, home or in the ministry, we find people who are under tremendous stress. Some are due to passionate ventures for finances. There's nothing wrong with ventures for financial gain but, it can cause stress when it is done without knowledge. The effects without knowledge are in most cases, financial instability. We also can find others who are passionate about their shopping and live above their means. They spend not only in the shopping malls but, on the Internet which creates serious debts. This is another destructive passion that causes stress, depression, and anxieties. These passions are done without counting the cost and will cost us, declining credit, destroy our family finances, and ultimately cause health problems. In serious cases, the individual should seek medical attention such as, counseling or psychotherapy.

In life, all of us have experienced disappointments caused by unexpected circumstances. A circumstance is a sudden turn of events that are beyond our control. Usually, one affects the other and it takes on a domino effect such as, death of a husband/wife; one dies and the family's income is now in jeopardy. Other examples are, bad weather occurs and one's plans have to be changed. Health conditions such as, Multiple Sclerosis, Brain Trauma, Rheumatoid Arthritis are very debilitating conditions that will affect our everyday living. The domino effect of a circumstance can place our passions on hold and even deny our privilege to pursue our passions depending on the severity.

In our everyday lives, we make decisions for all sorts of problems. One of our problems is called an issue. Issues are concerns that can be resolved with great effort for instance, issues between people that disagree on a certain point. Issues can also be conflicts that we fight to resolve within ourselves such as, sexual and emotional abuse, that effect our behavior. Issues are a part of everyday life. We can find daily issues on our jobs, family life, and ministry. Issues are a challenge to daily living because of the difficulty in obtaining a solution to the conflicts. Pursuing your passion can be delayed and even denied because of the duration of an issue.

The key factor in pursuing our passions is remaining focused but often we are distracted by circumstances and issues. I remembered wanting to get my degree but placing my focus on a man, I found myself with a baby instead of a degree. I enjoyed the process of making a baby but my passion was left behind. Some of us have lost love ones and passion died with them. Others found love, marriage, then the children came and our passions were swept under the mat of issues. Passions can be delayed or unfulfilled because we become preoccupied with issues and circumstances that we lose focus of our passions.

There is one passion that was placed in my heart by an invisible God. I took note of it while reading the Bible. It was a strange thing but I found myself writing when I happened to notice a topic that I found amazing. I enrolled myself at my local Bible School with a new desire to complete what I started writing. However, I realized that I was not in control. It appeared as though I was making the moves but there was someone working behind the scene, shifting gears and driving me like an automobile. He was placing His passions in the transmission of my heart. He was doing the steering, driving, and paved the way by the use of His Word. His intention was to lead me into my destiny.

Now, Passion is a motivator, whether healthy or

destructive, in the form of an activity, person, or a concept. It will create, and improve on whatever we enjoy or strongly believe in. It can be delayed and even unfulfilled due to circumstances. We often lose our focus and our passions are denied because of the issues of life.

But the passion placed in the heart by God cannot be denied because you're not in control. Your circumstances and issues are dealt with by God. We are steered and divinely driven by God, who holds you captive by His word and love. He paves the way for the completion of His passion placed in the heart. The Bible says in **Jeremiah 29:11 "For I know the thoughts that I think toward you, says the Lord, thoughts of peace and not of evil, to give you an expected end."** His expected end is called destiny. Destiny is where God created us to be. It's the place of fulfillment, joy, and doing everything that you were designed to do with ease. That's where I want to be! Smack dab in the middle of ease!

CHAPTER 2

"If I Can Say It, I Can Read It.
If I Can Read It, then I Can Write It"

In my Faith statement, "If I can say it, I can read it. If I can read it, then I can write it." I thought that it was a riddle. I was at my wit's end! What shall I say or read to cause me to write? I couldn't figure it out. So, I inquired of the Lord, and He blew life into my riddle. He said, "Diana, it's in your **IF**." It didn't make any sense; so I dared to walk around the house saying, "If I can, If I could, If I should, and what If I did?" To my amazement, I heard a noise and the sound of it was of a choice. That's what gave direction to my riddle. It's all about the path that we choose, and the treasure that keeps the heart focused!

The heart has to choose the path to get to the treasure that is for eternity. What's a Biblical treasure? There is a gift from God which is the Treasure of treasures. Believing ignites Faith. How do we work faith? What is a provisional statement? It's all about making a decision before your "**IF**" to cause an outcome.

The Bible is a Treasure Hunter's map that is full of choices. It's in the Bible that you can find roads that can take you on an easy journey to Hell, or a small road with a narrow gate that leads to Heaven. The easy journey to Hell is only for a moment, then the end of that journey is a dead end street. There will be no hope, no opportunities, only misery, wailing, and gnashing of teeth. On the other hand, to make it to Heaven, we have to go against the world system, for example, Salmon going upstream to spawn their young. It's a tough road, yet we are able to make it with a loving Savior and a multitude of host cheering us on. For the Bible says in **Hebrews 12:1 "Wherefore seeing we also are compassed about with so great a cloud of witnesses, let us lay aside every weight, and the sin which doth so easily beset [us], and let us run with patience the race that is set before us."** It's all in the volume of the book.

Some people will say that a treasure is a chest filled with all kinds of gem stones. Others will say that a treasure is the largest amount of currency. The Webster dictionary defines treasure as: ***1.** something of great worth or value; 2. a person esteemed as rare or precious, 3. **a** collection of precious things. Most people are hoping for a treasure chest to fulfill some lack in the physical realm.* The Bible clearly defines that there is a treasure in heaven for everyone that would believe on the gift that God gave to mankind for his redemption. For the Bible says, He is the door, and the light; everyone that comes to the Father must come through Him. If He is your treasure, (**focus**) you will have treasure here on earth, and eternity.

Unfortunately, most people are focused on the treasure of this world, and not on the treasure of treasures in heaven. For the Bible says in **Mark 8:36 "For what shall it profit a man, if he shall gain the whole world, and lose his own soul?"** There is a Treasure of Treasures who is a friend that sticks closer than a brother and one that laid down His life for you. It's rare, precious, and worth more than the largest gem. He's a friend that you can call in the midnight hour. That's priceless! A treasure is the one that leaves a lasting impression on the heart. For example, the Bible said in, **Isaiah 53:4 and 5 "Surely he hath borne our griefs, and carried our sorrows: yet we did esteem him stricken, smitten of God, and afflicted." "But he was wounded for our transgressions, he was bruised for our iniquities: the chastisement of our peace was upon him; and with his stripes we are healed."** This is the Treasure of Treasures that is wrapped up in human form and named Jesus. He who was, who is, and shall always be the King of

Kings and the Lord of Lords.

During the ministry of Jesus, He told a rich young ruler to give up his wealth and follow Him. Jesus knew that his treasure (*focus*) was not Him. The Treasure of Treasures is what leads us to the treasure storehouse in Heaven. Without Him, we cannot obtain what God had planned for us in his original creation. That's what the Treasure Hunter's map does; it leads the soul (**mind**) in the right direction; so that the heart (**spirit)** will believe, then the good measure of faith will take over.

We have to dig deep into the words enclosed in the volume of the book to disclose treasures in heaven that are accessible to us on the earth. For instance, the Bible says in **James 1:17 "Every good gift and every perfect gift is from above, and cometh down from the Father of lights, with whom is no variableness, neither shadow of turning."** Everything that one can desire or endeavor, there are laws and principals to get it to manifest in your life. One must believe in the Treasure of Treasures, and say it, then faith will be ignited. If I can read my corresponding scripture with an understanding, then I can work faith to get an outcome. For the Bible says in **James 2:26 "For as the body without the spirit is dead, so faith without works is**

dead also."

How do we work our faith? We work faith by going in the direction that we are believing in. For example: if you are desiring a house and there are no funds, act on faith, and go looking for that dream house. If you believe, it will show in your actions. Faith is an action word that's ignited by what you believe.

In my Faith Statement, "If I can say it, I can read it. If I can read it, then I can write it," it's a provisional statement. A provisional statement is dependent on your decision beforehand to get an outcome. God often used the word **IF**, for instance, **2 Chronicles 7:14 "If my people, which are called by my name, shall humble themselves, and pray, and seek my face, and turn from their wicked ways; then will I hear from heaven, and will forgive their sin, and will heal their land."** The word "If" lets you know that you have to make a decision, and act on faith to make an outcome happen.

Consequently, "If I can say it, I can read it. If I can read it, then I can write it," it's a provisional statement. It should read: "I believe it, and if I say what it is that I believe; Faith is already at work." I can read the corresponding scripture for my situation. If I can read it with a revelation, then I can write, "**Lay not up for yourselves treasure upon the earth, where moth and rust doth corrupt, and where thieves break through, and steal. But lay up for yourselves treasures in heaven, where neither moth nor rust doth corrupt, and where thieves do not break through nor steal. For where your treasure is, there will your heart be also.**"

CHAPTER 3

Facing Our Fears

(The journey within)

What a world we live in! There is so much turmoil, uncertainties, and tragedies. Our concerns about the economy, our jobs, disappointments in our lives, war, and just a feeling of what's next! If we pay attention to all these things, fear will rise up and take control of our lives. The Spirit of Fear will grip us, and tie us up into knots so that we couldn't move from what we see before us. How can we conquer Fear when everything before us is set for our down fall? We have fears within and fears without. It all starts on the inside, and it will affect your life, if you let it!

Years ago, in the 70's-80's things were much easier. You could find jobs, affordable housing, and living was not as challenging as it is today. Our economy has failed us. The Dow Jones has failed us. Food, housing, transportation, and being able to pay someone to watch our children while we work, is at an all-time high. We are paying much more for everything, and find it necessary to work two jobs to try to maintain what we have, and still finding it impossible.

Looking at our present day, it makes me see how fear

would grip us because of all the negative factors that are displayed on a daily basis. We watch the News, read the Newspapers, and even closer, watch our neighbors lose their homes to foreclosures. It's hard to see these things and not become afraid! But there are all kinds of fears; one is a natural fear that protects us for example: Don't play with fire, don't go into the deep blue sea without a boat. The Bible also states, that there is the Fear of the Lord, which is a reverential fear (respect for God) and there's another kind of Fear which is called the **"Spirit of Fear."** The Spirit of Fear is the one that keeps us from obtaining new jobs, homes, and giving to others in need. It also gives you doubts about yourself, such as, acquiring degrees, learning how to drive, and the fear of heights, all phobias. The Bible says in **2 Timothy, 1:7 "He did not give us the spirit of fear but of power, and of love, and a sound mind."** Let me break it down in layman's terms: God did not give us the Spirit of **Timidity**, but of **Power** from on High, and of Love which protects our loved ones, He equipped us with a sound mind filled with the word of God so that we can make righteous judgments. We were taught to have natural fear for our own protection but the Spirit of Fear is not so easily conquered.

How do we conquer the Spirit of Fear? Let's go back to the scriptures. The first scripture is **2 Timothy 1:7**, where it states He gave us power. Power is defined in the Webster Dictionary as: synonyms POWER, ENERGY, STRENGTH -means the ability to put out effort or force. POWER applies to the ability to act, whether only possible or actually used <the king had the power to coin money> ENERGY applies to store-up power that can be used to do work <the sun could be a great source of new energy for us> STRENGTH applies to that quality which gives a person or thing the ability to put out force or to oppose another's force or attack <test the strength of this rope>. The Bible has many scriptures that are relevant to the word **Power** such as, the woman with the issue of blood. **Luke 8:46 "And Jesus said, somebody has touched me: for I perceive that *Power* has gone out of me."** The second scripture is **Luke 5:17 "And it came to pass on a certain day, as he was teaching, that there were Pharisees and teachers of the law sitting by, who were come out of every town of Galilee, and Judea, and Jerusalem: and the *Power* of the Lord was present to heal them."** This Power is from Heaven. It's called in the Greek "Dunamis" (δύναμις), which means, Power like Dynamite. With this same power, we can conquer our fears within and without. This Power is the Holy Spirit, who leads and guides us into all truth. For example: in **Acts 1:5 "For John baptized with water, but in a few days you will be baptized with the Holy Spirit."** It further stated, in **Acts 1:8 "But you will receive *Power* when the Holy Spirit comes on you; and you will be my witnesses in Jerusalem, and in all Judea and Samaria, and to the ends of the earth."** You see, you cannot conquer the Spirit of Fear by yourself. For the Bible says that it is not by might or by your power but by His Spirit.

Lastly, one must take hold of courage, which only comes from knowing the word of God and petitioning the Holy Spirit to give you courage. That's what it takes, Holy courage that gives you strength to go against the tides, and the winds that hit us in life. The Webster Dictionary defines *Courage* as: Etymology: Middle English corage "the heart as a source of feelings, spirit, confidence," from early Frenchcurage (same meaning), from coer "heart," from Latin cor "heart"--related to CORDIAL: strength of mind to carry on in spite of danger or difficulty.

Therefore, One can face your fears whether within or without by taking hold of the word of God and His Power.

You cannot conquer the Spirit of Fear without the Holy Spirit, especially in these last days where the Hearts of many is failing. It's a Supernatural **Power** but we have to request, and invite the Holy Spirit to give you courage to take on those fears that would hold you back. The Journey within is following the instructions of the Holy Spirit and not what you feel or think

CHAPTER 4

What Can You Do When You've Done All You Can?

(Just Stand)

You got to do something to make something happen! We've all heard this golden rule, and used it, and most of the time it works. But there are exceptions to the rule especially, when life hits you with a left hook. You know a left hook of issues, circumstances, and situations that arises in everybody's life. What do you do when you've done all you can and everything goes disarray?

I've always been the type of person to put my hand to the grind to ensure that everything goes smoothly. My hand would be on my children's life, and on anything that concern me such as, my job responsibilities, my husband's future, my finances, and our health. With my children, I guided them with suggestions and ideas in the direction that I felt would advance them in life. I've covered all the bases but life still came knocking at my door. Life delivered things such as, unemployment, health issues, and children who didn't follow my suggestions or ideas. My husband leaves home to find himself without thought of his children, home in foreclosure, a water bill, or an overgrown lawn that I will have to mow by myself. What more can I do when these situations hit me all at once. Most people know that these issues, circumstances, and situations can and do happen all at the same time.

There was a man with a similar situation, his name was Job. In the Bible the book of Job the first chapter, we can read that Job did all he could to live a righteous life. He had houses and pastures for his livestock. He was a wealthy man with 10 children. **Read Job 1:3 "He owned 7,000 sheep, 3,000 camels, 500 teams of oxen, and 500 female donkeys. He also had many servants. He was, in fact, the richest person in that entire area."** Job followed all the rules and even thought about sacrificing to God for his children, just in case they sinned against God. This was Job's regular practice. He covered all the bases. He did all that he could do but his story ended up full of pain and suffering. The Bible states that he pleased God and God protected Job and his family by placing a hedge around all that he had. In **Job 1:8,** it reads **"Then the LORD asked Satan, "Have you noticed my servant Job? He is the finest man in all the earth. He is blameless--a man of complete integrity. He fears God and stays away from evil."** Satan then asked God permission to harm Job. **See**

Job1:11 "But stretch out your hand and strike everything he has, and he will surely curse you to your face." God granted the Devil the opportunity to do everything possible except to hurt his physical body. **Job1:12 "All right, you may test him," the LORD said to Satan. "Do whatever you want with everything he possesses, but don't harm him physically."** Satan left the Lord's presence, and went to do what He does best, to steal, kill, and destroy everything Job owned including his ten children. Now I know that it seems like a hard thing to hear that God gave the Devil permission but there is something to learn out of His righteous judgment so take time to read the entire book to get a full understanding.

What happened to Job was a terrible thing and it happened right after each other. It's not too far from what we experience in our lives. Similar when we reflect back to our own health problems, and loss of family. We should follow his lead for Job's future was better than what happened in his past, even though he did not know that it was just a test. **(See Job 1:12)**. The Bible states in **Job 1:22 "In all this, Job did not sin by charging God with wrong doing."** He struggled to understand what happened when he did all he could do but he stood strong on God's word.

I used the story of Job to demonstrate that when you've done all you can do things happen! But if we stand on God's word even when we don't understand, God will see you through. Remember that God has a plan even through pain and suffering. It doesn't feel good but the end result will be double for your troubles. It's not just Job who suffered but we can use Joseph who was thrown by his brothers into a ditch and left for dead; or Moses, that was given away at birth, and many others in the Bible that suffered unexpected issues, situations, and, circumstances. Just stand on His faithfulness! It's just a test!

CHAPTER 5

Stop Dragging Your Feet!

(Procrastination)

"Stop dragging your feet" was what I heard my mother say often, during my early stages of life. It didn't make sense at the time, but it's something we all do! We procrastinate in matters that are detrimental to our lives. Yes, including you! The world is waiting on your decision and there you are dragging your feet. I wonder why we procrastinate. I figured it out but it's up to you to make the choice to act on your decision, to do what you must do.

Why do we drag our feet? There are several factors: laziness, fear, unbelief, and the failure to act on our decisions.

Earlier in my life, my Mother would ask me to clean up around the house. I remembered dragging my feet just because I didn't want to do it. I was lazy, and I just didn't feel like it. In the meanwhile, I delayed what I had to do and made the process harder on myself. The sun was shining and there I was still cleaning the house, instead of enjoying a beautiful day.

Now that I am older, and somewhat wiser, I still

procrastinate in a very different way. How often do we all do everything else besides what we have to face, deal with, or end. Some examples are: career change, sticking to a budget, or ending a bad relationship. There are several factors for procrastination. The first factor is Laziness. That's what I had when I was younger. What I call, the big "L" is what most of us use as an excuse, even when we are older. It's defined in Webster Dictionary as: Encourage inactivity, Sluggish, and Slow to move. Webster Dictionary defines Procrastination as: to put off intentionally/ habitually something that must be done. Sluggish and slow to move, walks hand in hand with to put off intentionally or habitually something that must be done. It's a perfect marriage! I can imagine, that laziness encourages procrastination by tell it, "Oh do it later!" Let's just lie around on the couch, and watch television until we fall asleep. Tomorrow will be a better day. Procrastination will agree by saying, let's just cuddle. Some people do this all the time, thus they never accomplish anything. The house is dirty, and the children are undisciplined. Your behavior is learned by your children who will in time, intentionally put off what must be done. So you see, what you do affects others around you. That's what most procrastinators do not realize. The world is waiting on your next move in life. The Bible talks about Laziness, and the procrastinator. It's found in **Proverbs 20:4 "The sluggard will not plow by reason of the cold; therefore shall he begin harvest, and have nothing."** In other words, when you are lazy coupled with Procrastinate you find reasons not to do what is important for your future, as well as influence those around you.

Do you remember your first lesson on riding a bicycle? I remember it as being a scary experience. Against all my fears, I persisted to get on that bike in spite of, all my bruises until I became an expert. Did you know that some people become afraid after falling, and never get back on the bicycle? Fear is also a factor that works along with procrastination. The Webster Dictionary defines Fear as: to feel fear in oneself, to be afraid or apprehensive. Fear can stop all your attempts to get ahead. The mind will control the body not to reach for what is possible with effort. Procrastination doesn't want to do what must be done in a certain time frame. It waits for the very last minute. Together, Fear and Procrastination are excellent co-workers. Fear says wait don't do it you'll get hurt, and procrastination says let's wait for tomorrow. Maybe, tomorrow we will both feel better and get it done.

Have you ever had someone make you a promise, and you really didn't believe that they would do as they promised? I know I have! In the past I had many promises made to me, and they never happened. Of course, this experience caused me to have doubts in promises. Unbelief is a major factor that functions well with procrastination. As a matter of fact, they are best friends. Unbelief is defined in Noah's Webster Dictionary as: The withholding of belief; doubt; incredulity; skepticism. How can unbelief work with procrastination? Let's use an example of a class assignment that requires research, and, then writing a term paper for a final exam. Some of us doubt ourselves to the point of not attempting to do the research. Of course, doubt is unbelief even if it's in you! Procrastination will allow unbelief to do the work and it will just comply with your doubts. It will put off intentionally what must be done. Another prime example is: A relationship that's just not working but they continue to stay in it, because they feel that they might not find a better person. Procrastination will agree with his best friend! That's why we find people who are unhappy, and remain in a bad relationship for years. The Bible also states that the children of Israel had

Unbelief which caused them to circle around the same mountain for 40 years. It stops what God has for us, and causes a curse to fall on you and your love ones.

Therefore, procrastination is never alone. It works alongside others such as, laziness, fear, and unbelief. To avoid procrastination, you have to make a decision to act on what you must do right away. It's better to get it out of the way before other factors step in (laziness, fear, and unbelief) to comply with procrastination. The world is waiting on you! "Stop dragging your feet" is all about you recognizing why you procrastinate. Make a decision to act despite of your feelings. Your response affects others! In the book of **Proverbs 6:6-9 "Go to the ant, thou sluggard; consider her ways, and be wise. Which having no guide, overseer, or ruler, provideth her meat in the summer, and gathereth her food in the harvest."** Consider your ways, be wise, and change!

CHAPTER 6

Where is He When I Need Him?

(Perception)

In this life, we can go through so many situations, and circumstances. We experience tragedies such as, loss of jobs, homes, health issues, and death. We pray, go to church and try to keep the Ten Commandments. Still, there are times though unsaid, that we wonder where God is when we need Him. It's not a surprise, for most of us perceive God as the God who shows up when and where we desire Him to be. Our perception of God is that He is there to serve us instead of us serving Him. This is especially true when we are experiencing difficult times. God is our help in times of troubles but He doesn't always come the way we expect him too.

What is a perception? How does God operate? Is God concerned about our troubles? Our perception is at work in the time of trouble. Why would a loving God ignore us? Pain and suffering causes an effect to happen.

Growing up, one of my favorite shows was "I Dream of Genie." It was about an Astronaut who found a Genie in a bottle. He didn't want to believe it at first but she proved herself to him. The show was comical because the Astronaut kept trying to get rid of her due to the fact she often messed up his wishes. The Genie and the Astronaut loved each other in a strange way. I believe that most of us have a relationship with God and it's pretty much the same as the Astronaut and the Genie in the bottle. I can only explain this type of relationship through the "Perception Process" of the ***Who***, ***What***, and ***When*** that dictates **God's role in our lives**.

The "Perception Process" is defined: *1. as the process of using the five senses to acquire information on the surrounding environment or situation. 2. results of the process of perception, for example: The farmer planted a seed, and watched it grow, then noted his perception (idea) of how to grow an ear of corn. 3. impression: an attitude of understanding based on what was observed or thought. 4. the powers of observation: the ability to notice or discern things that escape most people. 5. psychology: neurological process of observation and interpretation: "Any neurological process of acquiring and mentally interpreting information from the senses."* www.bing dictionary. These definitions describe the human senses that allow us to perceive an understanding of the, **Who, What,** and the **When** of a situation.

How does God operate? He is a Spirit and the Bible says that His thoughts are higher than our thoughts. We must first recognize that God operates in the invisible. He sees the past the present, and the future. We need to acknowledge that there is a spiritual side that doesn't operate as our human perception process. There are Laws that govern the supernatural. Some of the Supernatural Laws are: the Law of sowing and reaping, the Law of confessing God's promises in our lives. As Humans, we use our perception process and the Laws that govern this earthly experience, and it hinders the supernatural manifestation that can assist us in our situation/circumstance. God allows us to see glimpses of the future without telling us what will happen in between. Our everyday experience only allows us to perceive what is visible to the human eyes. It's hard to see in the spirit when you're in panic mode. I don't care who you are, we all panic when the walls are caving in. That's why we have to remain in the spirit by reading God's will and being in constant communication with God.

In difficult times, we can make wrong choices by not consulting God first. By not relying on God's judgment we can find ourselves in even deeper troubles. God is concerned with all our troubles. We have to remind ourselves that he cares for us according to the Bible in **1 Peter 5:7 "Casting all your care upon him; for He careth for you."** It's all about us simply trusting Him. If you're not in a relationship with God, He still looks out for you. Have you ever found yourself in a situation and somehow got out of it? The unknown is the **Who**, which is (***God***) that got you out of your troubles. We can find examples of God's mercy, **Matthew 5:45 "That you may be the children of your Father who is in heaven: for he makes his sun to rise on the evil and on the good, and sends rain on the just and on the unjust."**

Unfortunately, life can hit you with circumstances that are beyond your control. That's when we turn to God and ask for help! We rub the bottle in hopes that He would grant us our wishes. There have been times when God was not perceived to my human senses. I didn't see, feel, hear, or touch Him anywhere in my life. It seemed as though He disappeared as I continued spiraling down in my circumstance. Whatever the situation, I know you've been there at that place of total hopelessness. Reaching for God and asking Him to turn your situation/circumstance around.

God never answered and your world turned upside down. Where was He when I needed Him? Why did He allow this situation to get to the worse when I called Him a long time ago? These questions arise with the emotion of anger associated with this kind of response from God. It comes when we expect Him to do as we prayed. I rubbed the bottle of prayer and the Genie never came out. My perception in the time of trouble is I need help and I need it now!

Why would a loving God ignore us? What came to my thoughts was the story of Lazarus, who was sick unto death and Jesus took His time coming to his rescue. Lazarus died 4 days in the grave. His sister told Jesus, if you had been here Lazarus would still be alive but I know I'll see him in the resurrection. In **John 11:25 "Jesus said unto her, I am the resurrection, and the life: he that believeth in me, though he were dead, yet shall he live."** He called Lazarus from the grave and Lazarus came forth from death, and the grave. I believe that one of the reasons God waits so long to come to our rescue is so that you and everyone else would know that He's the God of the impossible.

Furthermore, in pain, suffering, and the loss of a love one causes an effect to happen. We all have a gift on the inside that requires a shove, and a pulling out. Let me use a story from the Bible as an illustration: **John 9:2-3 "and his disciples asked him, saying, Master, who did sin, this man, or his parents, that he was born blind?" Jesus answered, "neither hath this man sinned, nor his parents: but that the works of God should be made manifest in him."** I'm sure that the man's life changing experience gave him a different perception of Who, and When God can do a miracle. Now the healed man's gift was revealed for the world to see, and he no longer had to beg for a living. Human perception, would say why let someone suffer to give God glory. The Bible says in **Philippians 2:13 "For it is God which worketh in you both to will and to do of his good pleasure."** Who are we to tell the creator what to do, who to use, and when to intervene. After all, can He not see everything from the end before the beginning? Selah.

Consequently, God is there in the time of trouble but He doesn't move in our time frame. His perception is far more superior. He sees the past the present, and the future, and ascertains Who, What, and When. If we could just wait on God everything will work out. He never told us that we wouldn't have troubles but He did say that He would deliver us out of them all. We have to continue to do our part by walking in faith. Furthermore, if you don't know Him be reminded that you can't live like Hell, and expect all of Heaven to help you! We must do our part!

CHAPTER 7

You Can Have What I Have

(Jealous/Envy)

Have you ever wondered why some people become angry when you enter a room? You didn't come in late or make any loud noises to attract attention but somehow, all eyes were on you. It could be that their envious or jealous of how you look! You know those people that for no apparent reason appear angry and disappointed that you came. While others, are jealous, envious of your status in life, your ministry, job, or the relationship you have with your children. They want what you got! They can have it; but they have to pay the price just like you had too! It's all about the eyes, and the mind!

Pretty girls have it hard. Society gives us the wrong impression by using the media. This impression was cunningly placed to give you the feeling that you don't have what it takes. What is the difference between jealousy and being envious? People can be envious, and jealous of many things, it all depends on their mindset. What is a mindset? It appears that some people don't have to struggle. With God, we can obtain our secret desires.

I have to say that my Granddaughter is gorgeous, and I am very happy to have her in my life. I try my best to toughen her up for the cruel world we live in. She's so innocent that she doesn't understand what I am trying to teach her. It will take some time before she gets the hard cold facts of life especially, being a pretty girl. The world is cruel all by itself but when society leads people to believe that they have a reason to feel inadequate; it can get out of hand! I say this because most people believe that pretty people get preferential treatment and that life is easier for them. It's not true! Most pretty girls have it even harder, for example: They have to deal with people who think they have better opportunities, thus causing "Pretty Girls" to be ridicule. They get hurt emotionally and have to hold their tears from the cruel mistreatment of others such as, family members, co-workers, strangers, and classmates! It takes a toll on a pretty girl especially, when she doesn't know why.

This society, has esteemed pretty people as objects to be worshiped. You see them in magazines, television, and the first person you see in a Business setting. The world says that your appearance is important more so than what you know. At least, that's what they portrayed to the public eye. This only establishes the feeling of jealousy, and envy. It gives children, as well as adult's the feeling of not having the right qualifications to compete with Society's view on how pretty people carry and conduct themselves. It's all about the eyes! Just as the ear gate goes to the heart of a person so is the eyes used to contact the heart. This is why sexy women and men are used as a visual tool on television to cause people to be sexually active. The eyes are also a gate to the heart where man makes decisions.

The truth is that society has it all wrong! This method of thinking was cunningly designed centuries ago by the rulers of this world. The Bible says in **Ephesians 6:12 "For we wrestle not against flesh and blood, but against principalities, against powers, against the rulers of the darkness of this world, against spiritual wickedness in high places."** Jealousy and envy are mindsets that were designed to influence your thoughts about yourself. It gives you the feeling of not having what it takes to get ahead in life thus adding the thought that you can't obtain what others have. It's not how you look but it's about what you're made of! What I mean when I say, it's what we are made of is: It's all about what's on the inside that appears on the outside. Have you ever met a person whose appearance was beautiful and when they open their mouth to talk the person becomes "Ugly" by the words that come out. Yes, it is what's on the inside that makes us beautiful. There is hope for change for the jealous/envious person by using the Bible to retrain our minds to think as God thinks of us. For the Bible says in **Romans 12:2 "And be not conformed to this world: but be ye transformed by the renewing of your mind, that ye may prove what is that good, and acceptable, and perfect, will of God."** We were created to give God glory and to fulfill His plans and purposes.

The Webster Dictionary defines Jealousy as: feeling or showing an unhappy or angry desire to have what someone else has. Envy is defined as, the feeling of wanting to be at a certain position in life that another has already reached. Both jealousy, and envy wants what another person has, but jealousy gets angry or unhappy because you have it or that it doesn't have full procession of it. It is fear that puts jealousy in motion. Envy is more of a discontentment of where that individual arrived in life. In other words, the person becomes envious because the individual see's where they should or could be. It's all designed to keep your eyes, and mind, off of what God thinks of you. The Bibles says in **Genesis 1:27 "So God created man in his own image,**

in the image of God created he him; male and female created he them." I don't believe that He created any of us as "Ugly." We were formed in His image. In my mind's eye, I don't see God the Creator of the Universe as "Ugly." I see Him as the most beautiful person both internal, and external.

People can also be envious and jealous of your ministry, status in life, and even of your relationship with you children. It's all about the other person's mindset. It could be something they were taught earlier in life or simply an idea that was portrayed by the media. Our eyes and minds are open to all kinds of satanic forces thus creating mindsets that are deadly to us, as well as others. It's just like the Devil to use all gates to the heart. For in the Heart is where things grow and begin to manifest to the surface of people, and it can get quite ugly. The Bible gave an example of jealousy: when it talks about King Saul who had disobeyed God and displeased Him, then God anointed David King to rule Israel. A little song caused King Saul to be enraged with Jealousy. The song is written in **1 Samuel 18:7 "This was the song "Saul killed his thousands and David his ten thousands!""** The Bible says that this made Saul very angry. It went into his ear gate and entered his heart. Instead of King Saul embracing David He began to devise ways to kill David. David respected King Saul even unto his death. Despite of God's judgment on Saul, Saul had the opportunity to rectify his disobedience to God by embracing David and helping him learn the mistakes that he made. The word of God is a tool to renew negative thoughts that enter the Heart through our eyes, and ears. All negativity will disperse by the revealed word of God. It's a process but it can be done. After entering the Heart whether it is visually, or through the ear gates it will become a mindset. We do have to make the choice to follow the guidelines in the Bible to overcome these worldly emotions.

What is a Mindset? The World Dictionary defines it as: the ideas and attitudes with which a person approaches a situation, especially, when these are seen as being difficult to alter or obtain. As Human Beings we often get stuck on mindsets that were embedded through the media, family or just what we pick up through our perception process. We tend to stay stuck in our ways of thinking until a word from the Lord shakes us loose. The Bible says that we should wash ourselves with the water which is the Word. It will replace all negative emotions of not being able to obtain what others have. The truth is clearly written in the Bible when it states I can do all things through Christ who strengthens me. We cannot restructure our thoughts in our own strength! That's the key, Christ the living word, and the relationship you have with Him. It's the Father's good pleasure to give you the desires of your heart even the secret ones. You can have what I have but are you willing to work, and exercise patience?

I have to agree that sometimes it appears that some people don't have to work hard to get what they have. It almost seems effortless on their part. While others struggle with everything they do. I know that's true in my life. Over the years I've noticed that whatever it is that I struggle to obtain I get it with extreme effort, but no one is able to take it from me. It's mine and if they do, I get it back even better the second time around.

Consequently, you and I are constantly, swayed to and fro from the struggles of life, the media, and what was taught to us as children effect our spiritual growth. It's important to read what God thinks of you and hold on to it. He thinks the best of you! He knows all your imperfections, and all He sees is the beauty on the inside that will reflect the majesty of His Son to this world. With God, we can obtain our secret desires through His preferential treatment for His children. Retrain your mind by reading, and hearing what God has for you. Keep up a positive mindset by using what God thinks of you.

CHAPTER 8

Do You Know What Kind of People are in There?

(Why we should go to church)

I pray, I keep the Ten Commandments, I pay my tithes, and I love everybody. But I am not going to church with those people. I've been there and done that. I know what goes on in there! Fake people, and then, there's the Church Mouse. No! No, I am not going there! I'll worship at home where I am safe from church goers.

How could anybody leave the church to serve God at home? Who is the church mouse? Jesus asked me three times. It's all about Jesus and not about the fake people or the church mouse!

What is going on with people that believe their better off worshiping at home? Now, I'm not talking about people who are bed bound but those who can walk, and communicate with others. I am really talking about myself! I did it for many years. I stayed home with my Television Evangelist, sent my tithes, and kept it moving. I did it because of my past experiences with Church Goers. Not all people in church are cruel but the few that are, make the good pay for the bad. It's easy to stay home, and worship; I don't have to deal with people, and their attitudes, or their self-righteous behaviors. After all, my relationship with Jesus was fulfilling with all the comforts of home.

Who is the church mouse? That's the person that knows everybody's business. The Gossiper, who goes from corner to corner, spreading all that she knows. She is the killer of relationships. Who wants to be around a mouse? You can't run from the church mouse because there is one, if not more in every church! It's much easier when it's Jesus and me. He is the keeper of my secrets.

One day while fasting, and praying, I heard from the Lord. Guess what Jesus said? He told me to "go to church!" I asked Him if He knew what kind of people are in there. He insisted "go to church." Why Lord, I don't want to be around those people! He said if you don't go, I can't talk to you anymore. Why not, I exclaimed? There's nothing wrong with our relationship! Why should I go back to Church with those fake people? He said three times, "Go to Church," and I finally thought I better listen because talking to Jesus was important to my life. So, I did as He told me.

Later, I found several churches to go too. I was torn between two churches; one was Prophetic and the other taught Biblical principles. I enjoyed both, and found it hard to join one. I still had Jesus and He never said anything to me about being committed. Maybe, He thought it was a bit much to ask, knowing what I've been through. That's what I still struggle with being committed. It's hard, after all my bad experiences lead me to this place of resistance. You see, you can go to church and ignore the church mouse with the fake people. I only attended church because Jesus asked me too. Did I like it? I enjoyed it very much. I just went for the Word, and took what I needed and left. I was still at home watching my Television Evangelist in my mind.

Jesus was pleased and continued our relationship in spite of my resistance to people! I suppose He really knew what kind of people went to church, but most of all, what was in me. I thought that I was different from the Church Goers but I was just like them. They all gathered at that place because Jesus brought them there to join them as one body in worship. As I looked back, I saw myself, and remembered where He brought me from. I was not a perfect person and I still have many imperfections. As I recalled, Jesus always hung out with imperfect people. The Bible says in **Luke 7:34 "The Son of man is come eating and drinking; and ye say, Behold a gluttonous man, and**

a winebibber, a friend of publicans and sinners!" He came to show us the way to an abundant life. He said, if you love me do as I say, and follow me.

Therefore, Jesus stated in **Mark 8:34 "And when he had called the people unto him with his disciples also, he said unto them, whosoever will come after me, let him deny himself, and take up his cross, and follow me."** Taking up your cross of imperfections, gossiping, putting on masks, bring it to him. We have to deny ourselves, which means overlooking what people do, and follow Him the author, and finisher of our faith. We have to live like Jesus and live the word. Be reminded that the Bible states in **Romans 10:14 "How then shall they call on him in whom they have not believed? And how shall they believe in him of whom they have not heard? And how shall they hear without a preacher?"** If we keep Jesus in front of us and our eyes on Him, and not on what people do, we can overcome! Church Goers and the Church Mouse are people who are a mirror of what we use to be. We must tolerate each other so that we can transcend to the level Jesus wants us to be. It's all about Jesus, and our relationship with Him. He forgives us all!

CHAPTER 9

In the Last Hours

(How God shows up)

Life has so many uncertainties, and circumstances. One of mines was losing my job in a recession. I was living off of unemployment for over a year. I lost everything I acquired over the years, such as, my apartment, my furniture, and having the resources to help not just my family but my friends. During this period of my life I found myself dislocated and seemingly alone. I soon learned that people didn't want to be around me because of my situation. It's a hard thing I suppose to be confronted with the possibility that the person in front of you could be you. I even thought that God forgot me, until He showed up in the last hours.

Here I was fifty one years old without a job. Worked all my life and suddenly there was a dramatic change in the way that I lived. I tried my best to cope with my circumstance. Unfortunately, it wasn't enough; I found myself homeless and having to live with family. My living arrangements with family didn't turn out so good, and I found myself moving once more to my son and his wife's residents. Thank God for children! We live together and try our best to coincide in a two bedroom apartment with a family of six. We do it well in spite of all our different personalities'.

Of course, they had their own problems, and I felt helpless. You see, I was always the person you could rely on in your time of need. I was no longer able to stretch my hand to even assist my family in their situation. Now their problem was also mine because they were about to be evicted. They were behind in their rent. It's a story that I am all too familiar with. The Landlord was kind hearted, and gave them time to get help and things fell apart. An Eviction notice was once again at their door. This time the Landlord refused to give them any more time and insisted that they pay their arrears. My family of course, was devastated, and I made arrangements to move in with a friend. My daughter in law and I often talked about all that she did to get help. I saw how she and my son struggled to get help. They just couldn't afford the rent. There I was again, unable to help, and now I too was being evicted once more.

During this particular circumstance, I called my local church for prayer and they prayed for the reversal of our eviction. They didn't pray that we get a new place but that the eviction would be reversed. I also heard the Lord say, "I am able." It's a strange thing but when you're going through your circumstance, you don't remember these prayers or the answer from the Lord. All I saw was us being thrown in street by the City Marshalls. The Landlord expected us to come with a sum of **3,475.00**. I made every effort to get this amount. To everyone that I asked it was as though I was asking for a million. No one could help us, not friends, co-workers, or Loan companies. We lost faith and my Son rented a storage facility as well as asking his friend to come over and help him. We were all planning our exodus.

Even though, all my friends were unable to help they listen to my plight. I had several friends that I knew for years from working with them, and I often told them what my family and I were going through. But there was one particular friend I called all hours of the night because she was a good listener. All I needed was someone to vent to. One day I came home only to see my Daughter in Law crying; it hit her that her three children would be affected by this sudden event. I tried to be strong but all I saw was gloom and doom. I left the house, and said in my mind

"Lord, please let the money come into my hands." I called that particular friend who was a good listener to say my good byes. I told her that I tried with no avail and in two days from now I will be traveling to another state; and I will stay in touch. She started crying, and said, "Diana I am your last hope." Then I asked her, "What do you mean?" She answered, "I will lend you the money that your family needs." I shouted for joy because the Lord had answered my prayers! It reminded me of when the Children of Israel reached the Red Sea and saw no way out. It's a miracle that delivered them and that's exactly what I got! You see, God touches and changes people's hearts. I never expected this to happen just like Israel didn't expect the sea to part and allow them to walk on dry land. In the last hours, God reversed the plans of the enemy on my family as He did when Moses stretch his staff over the Red Sea.

Sub-consequently, God shows up when we give up! Everything was arranged for us to leave and God step in. He can work a miracle whatever your situation or circumstance maybe. He's the God who shows up in the last hours, when it seems as though there is no way out. He still works miracles today. He always shows up when everything seems impossible!

CHAPTER 10

Betrayal

(How to Overcome)

One of the greatest treasures in life is a true friend. A true friend is like a good pair of shoes that never hurt your feet. Unlike a pretentious friend, who only looks like a pair of pretty shoes, but when you put them on for a while they give you corns. Friends lift you up and carry you until you're able to stand. Friends that are pretentious are only there for your destruction. Both are used by God to get you where God wants you to be.

What is a true friend? What is the intention of a pretentious friend? God uses every bad situation and turns it for your good.

Over the years, I've met many people but only a few friends. I can count them on one hand. A good friend will take time out of their lives to encourage you when you're down. They are there in good times and when life's storms come by. They last over the test of time. They are around for graduations, weddings, and know all your grandchildren. They are proud of all your accomplishments. A true friend will never let you down when you're at your lowest in life.

However, in life we meet many types of people, but there is one in particular that is cruel beyond measure. That's a pretentious friend, who appears as though they really care. You can be fooled by this type of person. They shine as angels of light and seem to be sincere by being there when you need them. They're hideous creatures with a bodysuit that wears like an angel.

Nevertheless, these pretentious angels of light are there to steer you in the right direction. Life sometimes sidetracks us from God's intention for our lives. God will use everything and every kind of creature to get you where you need to be. For example: Jonah was swallowed by a large fish but the Bible says that God had the large fish prepared to swallow Jonah to get him where He wanted him to be. The Bible states, that everything was made for His good pleasure. This includes true friends and, even the pretentious ones.

I met a few of these hideous creatures in my lifetime. How they pour the syrup on as method to draw information so they can devour you when they are ready. They just wait until they get enough information so that they can damage your character. It reminds me of Jesus and Judas Iscariot relationship. It's a familiar story to the saved and unsaved. How can one walk so close, see the miraculous, know that He's the Messiah, and sell Him out for *$30.00* worth of Silver. That's because He was a pretentious friend. He had to be! Such a betrayal comes from the heart. He didn't even stop to think about it. But God had a plan! He used Judas to turn Him over to the Jewish leaders, for he was the weakest link out of the twelve. The Definition of Betray in Webster is: *1. to lead astray; especially: seduce. 2. to deliver to an enemy by treachery. 3. to fail or desert especially in time of need, and 4. to reveal unintentionally, b: show, indicate c: to disclose in violation of confidence <betray a secret>*. To deliver to an enemy by treachery is what Judas accomplished and it appeared that Jesus was down for the count. God didn't pick Judas but Judas had it in his heart and God worked a bad situation to get Jesus to the cross where He would bear the sins of the world, and then become the Everlasting King of the world. There are many types of betrayals that are done in relationships, such as, the betrayal of trust for instance: a trust between a husband and his wife, who take vows to be faithful to each other and when the vow is broken it causes distrust. Two close friends that know everything about each other and a secret is revealed to others is a betrayal of confidence. Another form of betrayal is when one promises to do something and for no reason at all they don't. That is to fail in my time of need. Betrayal is one of the most hurtful experiences, and very difficult to overcome, especially when you believed that the person was a true friend.

How can one let go of what someone did to you? The first thing you must acknowledge that you didn't cause this on yourself. This kind of person had it in his/her heart a long time ago. Secondly, see God in the situation. Look back, cry, and then wipe your tears because God has a plan and a future for you. He uses what was meant to destroy you and will turn it for your good. Lastly, forgive that individual and move on, know that God said that vengeance is mine. Let go and let God do his part.

Consequently, God is in the midst of every betrayal. He understands how it hurts because it happened to Him. Just do your part and God will turn it for your good. His plan is to get you where you need to be. Trust Him to get you there in spite of the pain and the emotional trauma, because out of every painful situation comes something wonderful. The Bible says that weeping may endure for the night but oh joy is coming in the morning.

CHAPTER 11

Why are We So Easily Offended?

(How to overcome)

There are all types of people in the world. One type is passive; another is aggressive, while others are just used by the Devil. We were all put here on this earth to complete a purpose. God created all of us for His pleasure and to give Him the Glory. It makes life difficult when you have people who are used by the Devil to distract you off your course towards a godly lifestyle. It's a hard thing when you're lied on, betrayed, and mistreated. But through every offense know that there is a blessing that follows.

Christ is our example of suffering to be righteous although, none of us have suffered as Christ did but after His pain He received a crown. The Bible states in **Revelation 5:12 "Saying with a loud voice, worthy is the Lamb that was slain to receive power, and riches, and wisdom, and strength, and honor, and glory, and blessing."** The word blessing in this scripture is what we all want to acquire. Blessing is defined in the International Standard Bible Encyclopedia: (eulogia pneumatike): Any blessing administered in the realm of the spiritual life;

specifically the blessing of the Spirit in introducing the believer into "the heavenly places in Christ." **(Ephesians 1:3)**; a term expressing the fullness of blessing in God's gift of eternal life in Jesus Christ. The Blessing is mentioned in the bible for our health, favor with God and man. The Blessing is worthy of our focus instead of the lies, betrayals, and mistreatment by others. Just as God uses people, the Devil also has his people to sway us from the blessing.

How do we stay on course when we are easily offended? It's not an easy task because when we put our eyes on the individual who wronged us, we cannot see Jesus, then the offense is working. Let's use Jesus as an example: In **Luke 17:1 "Then said he to the disciples, it is impossible but that offenses will come: but woe to him, through whom they come!"** In this scripture He is preparing us for such offenses.

Why are we so easily offended? As Humans, striving to stay in the race of our salvation, we try to do all the right things and when we get mistreated and lied on we tend to stop and focus on the person. My reaction is I don't want to see the person ever again! It just hurts so bad that anyone would be so mean. But I am learning that it's not the person it's the Devil! He's the one that is chasing you off the road toward the blessing! I know I want the blessing that will overtake me. It just hurts so bad that I have to stop for a minute and re-group. For the Bible says in **Luke 6:35 "But love your enemies, and do good, and lend, expecting nothing back; and your reward will be great, and you will be children of the Most High; for he is kind toward the unthankful and evil."** We have to overcome those moments of despair and discouragement of people used by the devil by keeping our eyes on the blessing.

However, keeping our eyes focused on the blessing is not an easy task when our hearts are in pain. We have to get a tough skin my Mother would say! Sometimes we have to just ignore the pain and follow our eyes on the prize at the end of the road. The bible says that the race is not for the swift but to those who endure. Furthermore, this Godly life style requires discipline. Discipline as described in the scriptures in **Luke 9:23 "And he said to them all, if any man will come after me, let him deny himself, and take up his cross daily, and follow me."** Deny your hurts, pick up your own down falls, and follow Him. Keeping your eyes on the crown at the end of the road!

Therefore, one must overcome your own hurt whether

you're lied on, mistreated, or betrayed. For the Bible says in **Revelation 21:7 "All who are victorious will inherit all these *blessings*, and I will be their God, and they will be my children."**

CHAPTER 12

The Difference in God and Man!

(Love and Hate relationship)

Everything in life is not so simple! It's all about knowing the difference between what Man does to you and what God can reveal through his Law.

Everything in life is not so simple! There are conflicts within and conflicts without. Life gives you all kinds of disappointments, hurts and then the anger. Living our daily lives, we go through emotional abuse, heart breaks, health issues, financial situation, homelessness, and family turning on you. Whatever caused you to become bitter will cause you to put people and God in the same category.

How do we put God in the same Category? We do it without thought. Here's an example **1 Kings 19:9 "There he went into a cave and spent the night. And the word of the LORD came to him: "What are you doing here, Elijah?"** Elijah went in a dark cold cave by being disappointed that his efforts were not effective, and Israel killed all the prophets and now wanted to kill him too. This prophet of God had given up hope on people and lost faith that God was with him. Elijah was just a man with disappointments, hurts, and even some fear. He did exactly what we do! We run into our caves to get us away from people, and hide from God. We have to ask ourselves what brought us to this dark, cold place. Were you disappointed in people or yourself?

Life can serve you and unfair game of cards but it's not the game that gets us. It's how we categorize them. For instance, one cannot place every person and God in the same box. I have a saying that I tell people when their hurt, and angry at another. You cannot be angry at the Mother and take it out on the child. We have to see God as a different person and not put the blame on Him for everything that was done by people or the choices we make. Hurting people tend to categorize everyone as the same. Just because I'm angry at Sue doesn't mean that Sally is involved because she was present at the time of the incident. Just as we tend to blame God for everything that happens to us. People in general seem to think that God is in control of everything that people do. He gave man a free will. Man will always do what he thinks is right if he/she is not controlled by the Holy Spirit! God only moves when He sees faith in action. We have to differentiate what man does and what God does! Let's use Joseph the dreamer in the Bible. Joseph was just a young man telling his dream but his brothers were jealous of him and put him in a ditch. Man is full of cruel and evil emotions which cause them to make wrong choices. They have a free will to either live righteous or do evil. God only can do what his word declares. He will punish those who do evil. That's God's Law "Whatsoever a man sows so shall he reap."

What happens to the person whom evil touched? According to Law, God will turn this evil for the individuals good. We can see this law in effect in the book of Genesis where Joseph's brothers threw him in a ditch for dead, and God worked it for his good. God had a plan and future for Joseph and his entire family. If we continue to follow the law and shun evil, then God will work it for our benefit, as well as our family members. But we also have to consider that Joseph continued to obey God and His law to get what God had prepared for him. It's the same for us today; in spite of what people do we have to continue operating in God's Laws. God is not Man and we have to view Him separately from what is done to us by people. For instance: if you were abused as a child, raped, had a family member who was killed, whatever made you bitter, or disappointed God had nothing to do with it. He foresaw it but He only operates within His Laws and man has a free will! Many people consider God as the person that placed us in this earth and hold Him solely responsible. But the truth is God gave man dominion over the earth and man was supposed to go to God and ask Him what to do in everything.

Man chose to disobey God and this is why we live in a tragic world. Man made himself god and evil reigns. It's not hopeless because of Jesus Christ who gave us another opportunity to come boldly to the throne of Grace. We can still obtain God's consolation, but we have to keep in mind that God is not what Man does! Let's not categorize him in the same box as evil men, and blame him for something that man has dominion over. I also have to constantly remind myself that God is not what my Mother, brother, friend, or my Husband does towards me. Let's get our thoughts right! Life can make us bitter by all that we go through, but the Bible says in **James 1:17 "Every good gift and every perfect gift is from above, and cometh down from the Father of lights, with whom is no variableness, neither shadow of turning."** God is waiting on us to come to him for the solution in spite of what is occurring in our lives. He's waiting on you to believe that he is not the person that is hurting you. He's just trying to help you through it and make you the winner.

This book is composed of short stories that were written to give the reader a different perspective of God. It contains such stories such as, "Where is He when I need Him." It's a story based on emotions that we feel while we are going through extenuating situations. "How to Overcome Envy/ Jealousy" is based on emotions that are uncontrollable but can be worked on if you see yourself the way God see you. This book is full of real life experiences, and emotions that occur in a Christian's life. It will inspire people with a Christian lifestyle as well as captivate those that don't attend church but have a strong belief in God. My motivation is to get people to see God in real life situations. These stories were written in simplicity so that it can be applied to the reader's life. It contains scriptures to relate to situations that can occur in ordinary people's lives.

By Diana Stevens

About the Author

Diana Stevens is a single woman who was born in Panama City, Panama but was raised in Brooklyn, New York. She has one son and a granddaughter. She's a kind woman with a quiet demeanor, who worked as a secretary for over 21 years; in hospitals and nursing homes. Her interpersonal relationships with people caused her to realize that she had something inside of her when she began to write for other people. She never thought about writing a book but it was placed in her heart by God. Diana has had many life experiences where only God could have brought her out. Life is her teacher. God is her Creator, and deliverer.

www.ingramcontent.com/pod-product-compliance
Lightning Source LLC
Chambersburg PA
CBHW072107290426
44110CB00014B/1860